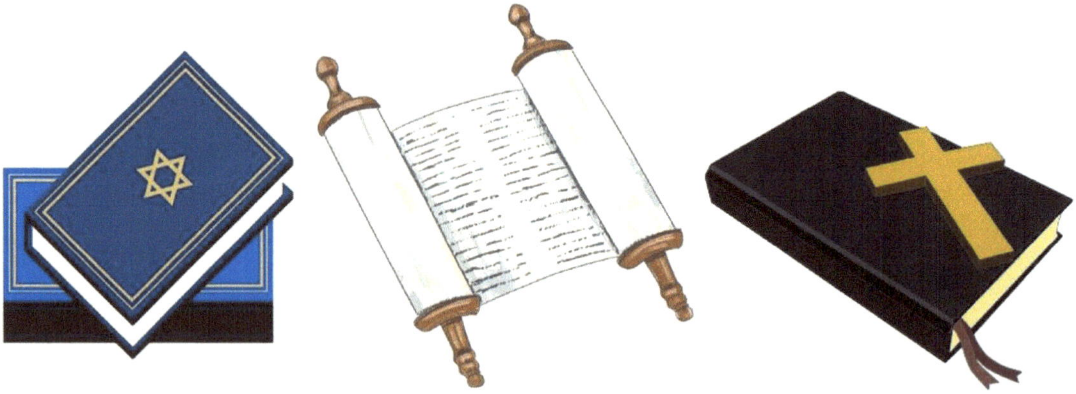

[C] 2018 CHELSEA KONG

ALL RIGHTS RESERVED. ALL IMAGES USED IN THIS BOOK ARE LICENSED COPIES FROM THEIR RESPECTFUL OWNERS INCLUDING PEXELS, PIXABAY, AND OTHERS. THIS BOOK OR ANY PORTION THEREOF MAY NOT BE REPRODUCED OR USED IN ANY MANNER WHATSOEVER WITHOUT THE EXPRESS WRITTEN PERMISSION OF THE PUBLISHER EXCEPT FOR THE USE OF BRIEF QUOTATIONS IN A BOOK REVIEW.

PRINTED IN 2019, MADE IN TORONTO, CANADA

Stay alone with God

God wants alone with Him every day.

David and Daniel were alone with God.

Look for a quiet place to be alone.

You will be closer to God when you spend more time with Him.

learn to Rest in God.

Pray every day

Prayer is talking to God, Jesus Christ, and the Holy Spirit every day about everything.

Pray His Word into your life.

Pray for others.

Pray in secret and with others.

Seek God

Seek God with all your heart, mind, and strength.

Seek His face and seek to know Him.

He wants to share His heart with us.

Worship

Worship is to love God with your whole heart, mind, and soul in all that you do

It is your spirit and soul speaking to God.

Worship brings glory and honour to God and it shows that we love Him.

It will make you smarter.

Ask what He means and write it down.

Sing songs and Praise

God loves it when we
sing songs to Him

He also loves it when
we play music and praise Him.

You can also sing in the Holy Spirit.

You can sing Psalms and Song of Songs.

Thanksgiving

Thank God for all that He has done, who He is, for His Word, and for everything!

Thank God every day!

Thank Jesus for dying on the cross for you

Thank the Holy Spirit for teaching you.

Pray by the Holy Spirit

Let God pray through you.

He uses our tongue to speak a language that somebody may know or a language from heaven.

 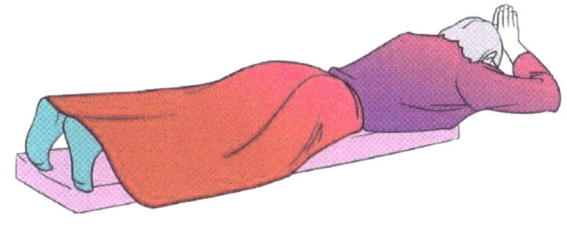 

He wants to speak His plans
and He will protect your future.

Wait and Listen

It also lets you speak to God
and for Him to speak to you.

He speaks in different ways to us.

Wait for Him to speak to you.

He wants you to take time to let Him speak to you.

We get changed when we spend time with Him.

Remember

Keep in your heart and mind.

Remember His word every day.

Think about it and remember Him.

Keep a copy of what He says

God may give you words, song, pictures, a dance, poem, idea

thought, feeling, and speak to you His word.

You can write, draw, sing, dance.

You can record what you hear.

Obey

Follow what God, Jesus, and Holy Spirit tells you to do because they are always right.

Do what His word says with a joyful heart.

Share with others

Share with others about Jesus to know Him.

Tell them that God loves them and wants to speak to them.

Make friends with others.

He also wants us to spend time with others.

Stay close to those who follow Him.

SALVATION PRAYER

God, I know I sinned against you. Forgive me for the wrong that I have done. I believe that Jesus Christ died on the cross for me. That He rose from the grave so that after three days. I can have His long-lasting life. Come into my heart to be my Lord and Savior. I choose to turn away from my sins and I choose to follow you. Lead me to walk with you. Keep me safe and teach me your ways. Stop every bad thing in my life that has an open door to hurt me. Close those doors. Holy Spirit fill me now in Jesus' name. Amen.

You now have a new life in Jesus Christ and live with God in heaven and on the earth.

He will teach you His ways as you stay with Him.

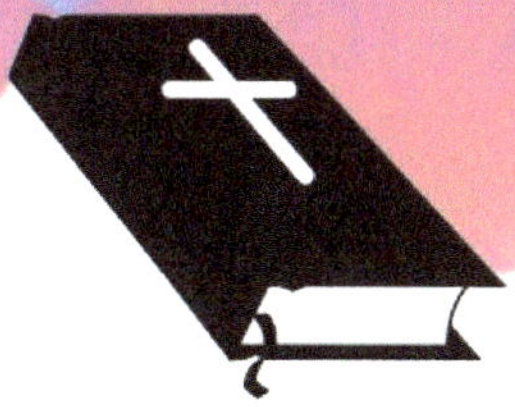

Make sure you go to church every week and spend time with God every day.

God loves you and wants the best for you.

BAPTISM IN THE HOLY SPIRIT

Jesus, you are the one that fills me with Your Spirit. Come Holy Spirit and come into my life and fill me to overflow with Your presence. Come with your fire too. Thank you for the gift of tongues in Jesus' name. Amen.

Open your mouth and let the words come out that God gives you. It will be words that you don't know what they mean. You can ask God what it means. You need to let Him talk through you every day to grow this gift.

He will bring you closer to God and you will know Jesus more. You will have power from God to do great things and know things.

PRAYERS

Father God, thank you for teaching me how to build a relationship with you. Help me to spend every day with you to know You, read Your Word, hear Your voice, seek Your face, and walk with You every day. Teach me Your word. Help me to pray in Jesus name. Amen.

PRAYERS

Father, Give me the strength to share with others about You. Make me smart, so that I can help others. Put Your love inside me to share with others. Give me a desire to want you more each day. Keep me safe from harm. Show me who I can become friends with in Jesus name. Amen.

Father, help me to be the light for You. Holy Spirit fills me and gives me the power to do God's work. Jesus, you are my best friend. Take my hand and lead my steps.

Thank you for teaching me your word. Thank you that you love me and thank you that you are with me always in Jesus' name. Amen.

BLESSING PRAYER

Father God, thank you for your children. Protect them and lead them. Guide their steps everyday to know You and to live for You. That they can make a different to those around them. That when people see them that they will be touched by Your Holy Spirit to know that they need You. That these children will have the power of the Holy Spirit to touch and change lives for Your glory. That they will impact generations and change systems for You. That the world will never be the same again in Jesus name. Amen.

Father, thank you that children are a reward from the Lord. That all Your blessings comes and that each of them will flow in Your power and anointing. That nations will shaken and people will awaken. That they will hear Your voice and know You. That they will become a mighty nation and a power house for the Lord God. That they will walk in faith and in the Truth all the days of their lives. That they would not be affected by the world, but impact the world. That people will know that their is a God and will desire You in Jesus name. Amen

Message from the Author

God put it in my heart to write this book to teach children how to build a relationship with Him. Many people have not been taught the importance of knowing God. It's His heart for people to be close with Him. He made man and woman have a close relationship with Him to show the world who He is. Children are powerful in the hands of the Lord and He doesn't want any of them to be taught by the world how they should be. That is to keep them pure and godly for Him to change the world that we live in, so that all mankind may know that there is a God.

OTHER PRODUCTS

- Knowing God
- How to Hear God's Voice
- New Life in Jesus
- Loving Israel
- God's Gifts
- Meeting God
- Word Power
- Fruit of the Spirit
- The Tabernacle
- Bride for Jesus
- A Life of Prayer
- Live Free
- Who am I in Jesus
- Walk in Love
- God's Favor
- Man of God
- Woman of God
- How to Use Money
- God's Wisdom
- Fasting
- See Jerusalem and Bethany
- First Fruit Offering
- Feast of Trumpets
- Day of Atonement
- Feast of Tabernacles
- Counting the Omer
- Glory, Presence, and Holy Spirit
- 31 Day Devotional
- Biblical Puzzle Book Vol 1
- Biblical Puzzle Book Vol 2
- Biblical Puzzle Book Vol 3
- Biblical Puzzle Book Vol 4
- Biblical Puzzle Book Vol 5

OTHER PRODUCTS

Teaching Series

How to Hear God's Voice Teaching Guide & Audio Book

Teaching (Non-Sale)

Purim

Passover

Resurrection

More books to come!

More books on Amazon, Kobo, and Barnes and Noble
https://chelseak532002550.wordpress.com/

Review

More books on Amazon, Kobo, and Barnes and Noble
https://www.amazon.com/author/chelseakong

Please leave a review and share with friends to help the author continue to write more books to reach more readers. Thank you so much for your support.

About
CHELSEA KONG

She is a writer, creative arts and digital media artist, skilled administration professional, and podcaster. Chelsea also served in a variety of roles, from audiovisual, photography, to assisting on the worship team, and ministry team. She also has a passion for families being united.

Chelsea has been a guest on Unity Live Radio and The Lady Tracey Show and is highly recommended by a Proud Christian blog. She graduated from Hotel and Restaurant Management, Digital Media Arts, Office Administration, and experience working with children. Chelsea lives in Toronto, Canada. She mainly writes children's books, stories, bridal writing, poems, lyrics for songs, words of encouragement, blessings, prayers, and jokes. The author of How to Hear the Voice of God, the Bridal Collection, Knowing God, etc. She also has her own Bible Puzzle books and other inspired products. Her podcast channel is called Chelsea K on Anchor, Spotify, and iTunes.

Please check my website to find out more:
https://chelseak532002550.wordpress.com/

www.ingramcontent.com/pod-product-compliance
Lightning Source LLC
Chambersburg PA
CBHW041417010526
44107CB00016B/1198